EDUCATOR'S JOB SEARCH

The Ultimate Guide to Finding Positions in Education

By Martin Kimeldorf

An NEA Professional Library Publication

This book is dedicated to all of the people who have helped me in my job search. Their interest, concern, and assistance were essential markers on my career pathway. I would like to name just a few whose help was long standing and invaluable: Judy, Jean, Al L., Jack, Joyce, Caleb, Tom, Richard, Don and Fay, Don G., Ben, Gaye, Kirby, Dave, Al B., Karen, Mark, OSU Placement Office, PSU Placement Office, relatives, neighbors, and strangers at conferences.—MK

Printing History:
First Printing: February 1993

Note
The opinions expressed in this publication should not be construed as representing the policy or position of the National Education Association. Materials published by the NEA Professional Library are intended to be discussion documents for educators who are concerned with specialized interests of the profession.

Library of Congress Cataloging-in-Publication Data
Kimeldorf, Martin.
        Educator's job search: ultimate guide to finding positions in education/ by Martin Kimeldorf.
                p.   cm.
        Includes bibliographical references (p.).
        ISBN 0-8106-1860-5
        1. Teaching--Vocational guidance--United States. 2. Teachers-Employment--United States. 3. School employees--United States. 4. Job hunting--United States.   I. Title.
LB1775.K546 1993
370' .23'73--dc20   93-380
                                     ® GCIU   CIP

CONTENTS

Preface

In 1982, during the previous recession, I stood in the unemployment line. I could not find a teaching job, or any other job for that matter. Right behind me stood some of my former students and teaching colleagues. It was the worst of times, but I knew then that there had to be a better way. Job searches and careers should not end in the unemployment line.

A Better Way

I was determined to find that better way. I read every book on job hunting I could find. I visited with experts, and I bartered my way into job-search conferences. Soon I began to see common patterns of behavior among successful employment agencies and job developers. It just so happened that at the same time these patterns were being formalized and codified into a new body of literature called *self-directed job-hunting tactics*.

The tactics were clearly effective. They were skills that every potential job hunter (i.e. student) should learn *before* entering the marketplace. But, like many social innovations, I feared the education establishment would be the last to find out about these important practices. I decided to attack that lag-time by creating a workbook that teachers could use to teach self-directed job-hunting tactics to their students. I called this workbook *Job Search Education*.

After the book was published, I was paid the highest compliment when Joyce Lain Kennedy, who writes the nationally syndicated column *Careers*, reviewed the workbook with these words:

> What the author has done is adapt sophisticated executive job-search strategies to benefit applicants for entry-level jobs. He's done it well; it's a lot of book for the money.

My life was changed by the publication of that workbook. I did not go back into the classroom for six years. During that time, I wrote several related books for students and worked on various projects that promoted job-search education.

On one project, I directed a national research program to train high school teachers, high school students, and graduate students in my techniques. It was an exciting culmination of my earlier efforts, especially when 80 percent of the high school students found jobs!

As that project wound down, I decided to write a book that summarized all of my research about job finding and to put it in a format that job-hunting teachers could use. Hence, *Educator's Job Search*, was born.

Several of the examples and sample resumes I use in this book come directly from the teachers and graduate students I worked with on the national research project (although the names have been changed).

A Job-Search Book for Teachers

The advice in the book works for all types of teaching positions. While most of the specific examples involve public school positions in grades K–12, they still can apply to all teaching jobs, including jobs at private colleges and universities.

Appendix A provides additional notes for those interested in college and university positions. And Appendix B discusses how to uncover overseas jobs in teaching.

You can even use the ideas in this book if you do not have teaching credentials. Every day, "laypersons" get hired via consulting contracts and grants to execute programs in schools. These people are hired for their talent first. Often, they fill positions in arts education, special vocational training, or community relations. To find these unusual or hidden opportunities, you have to dig. This book will show you how to do just that.

Looking Beyond the Obvious

It may not be 1982, but it's still very tough to get a teaching job. As a result, teachers have to learn more effective ways of finding job opportunities. We can all access the obvious or visible openings in college-placement offices, local school-district personnel offices, and classified ad sections. But then so can everyone else.

This book is about looking and going beyond the obvious. It encourages you to take the uncommon pathway to your next job. If you are ready for this challenge, then you will be rewarded with a quality job search.

A quality job search requires two things. First, it requires *time*. Are you willing to put time into polishing your job-search skills? Are you willing to spend a few hours each week writing letters, making phone calls, and researching potential work sites?

Second, it requires *risk*. Are you able to take the risk of being rejected—and then the challenge of persisting in the face of that rejection?

This book will not make your job search easier, but it will make it more effective. You will encounter tips and exercises to help you get a handle on your marketable skills. You will also learn how to locate valuable contacts and potential job sites through networking, how to develop a quality resume, and how to make a strong impression in job interviews.

In short, you will learn to become a self-directed job seeker. You will learn to rely first on your own efforts and secondly on the efforts of other people and organizations. In so doing, you will become known to the decision makers and the influential teachers of the school districts of your choice. You will become more than just another name in a personnel-office file. You will become a leading candidate!

Good luck in your job search.

—**Martin Kimeldorf**

INTRODUCTION

If you are a college student or are planning a job search in the future, don't put off reading this book. The exercises on the following pages take time, but through these exercises, you will learn how to:

- examine yourself—your strengths, weaknesses, past experiences, and goals;
- investigate school districts to see how they compare with your attributes and goals;
- network to discover leads and key contacts;
- write an impressive resume;
- give a great interview;
- effectively organize and maintain your job search; and
- thoroughly evaluate job offers.

If time allows, pace yourself through this book. Complete a few of the exercises each week. That way, your job search will not feel overwhelming.

This book is packed with information, all of which I believe is valuable. But if I were asked to identify four key job-hunting tips that I would like every reader to get from this book, they would be the following:

Job-Hunting Tip #1: *Champion your strengths.*

You need to be able to tell others about yourself. The best way to do this is to identify specific examples that speak to your aptitudes and qualifications.

You might want to compose an actual Work Strengths Summary (see Chapter 1) and use selections from it in your resume, networking activities, and job interviews.

Job-Hunting Tip #2: *Use back doors.*

Job seekers are always advised to go to the "front door"—to fill out a placement application via the personnel department and to read the placement bulletins. To get "inside," where the real decisions are made and the hidden opportunities exist, you need to enter a few back doors. Back doors include meeting teachers in the field, networking at conferences, and conducting career surveys with principals. Back-door people learn the language and aspirations of the school districts they are considering. They write resumes that sell themselves because they reflect the vocabulary and thinking of the district. In the end, back-door people know the most powerful job-search lesson of all: Aside from all the latest hiring fads and techniques, people still hire people. Hiring is tiring and grueling. If you make it easy by previewing your wares, you increase your chances of obtaining that all-important interview.

Job-Hunting Tip #3: *Think like an employer.*

Picture yourself making a tough hiring decision, worrying about the outcome and about not having enough time to do the hiring job right. Use this empathy to guess at how the hiring authorities will react to your resume, job-search style, interview answers, and networking.

Job-Hunting Tip #4: *Persist. Persist. Persist.*

Many teachers find it difficult to continually follow up during a job Often they feel that a second and third follow-up call will result in rejection or being perceived as "coming on too strong." My advice is to come on strong when your life goals are at stake. The world is busy, the hiring authorities are overworked, and the squeaky wheel often gets the opportunity. At worst, you will hear a simple "no," and at best, you will demonstrate your sincere interest in a particular school district. If, after two or three calls, the district continues to say, "we'll call you," then naturally, use some sensitivity, but never be timid!

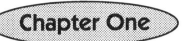

Chapter One

ASSESS YOURSELF!

Your first tasks as a job hunter are to determine what you want from a teaching job—your goals—and what you do best in teaching—your marketable skills, or work strengths. To make these determinations, you need to be able to answer that profound question: Who am I?

This section helps you recall past experiences in order to identify key words and specific examples that speak to your unique teaching goals and skills. It then helps you organize those words and experiences into a one- to two-page work-strengths summary that you will find enormously helpful when it comes time for job networking, resume writing, and interview preparation.

Describe Your Ideal Job

Job satisfaction depends on three factors: *job conditions*, such as the size, location, and nature of your work place; *job content*, such as what you do on a day-to-day basis and the areas of expertise you use; and *job compensation*, such as salary, health insurance, and retirement benefits.

The following exercise can help you determine conditions and content that are important to your job satisfaction. (We'll discuss compensation in a later chapter.)

1. My ideal job would be working with these types of students:

2. My ideal work setting would include (describe location, size, and philosophical environment):

3. In my ideal teaching situation, I would spend the majority of my day doing these things:

4. My fellow teachers would help me by:

CONTINUED ON NEXT PAGE ☞

5. I would enjoy the company of my peers while pursuing these things:

6. My principal or supervisor would say he or she appreciated this quality about me as a person:

7. My principal or supervisor would say he or she appreciated these teaching skills of mine:

8. My supervisor would show his or her support for me by:

9. I would spend extra time on:

10. Five years from now I see my job or career changing in this way:

Identify Your Work Strengths

A *skill* is any quality, body of knowledge, or ability that enables you to accomplish a task and produce a result.

The three exercises that follow help you identify your major strengths in each of these three skill categories.

Each exercise asks you to choose three or more words or phrases that describe you. Don't limit yourself to the choices on these pages. Feel free to add your own descriptions. If you are not sure how to identify yourself, ask people who have had a working relationship with you to help.

Part I: Qualities

Qualities are skills that describe the type of person you are. They are the personality traits and work habits you bring to any job.

Circle three to five words that describe your professional attitude, work habits, or interpersonal skills.

Initiating	Flexible	Cooperative
Mature	Organized	Independent
Reliable	Accurate	Receptive
Professional	Decisive	Friendly
Enthusiastic	Fair	Outgoing
Versatile	Adaptable	Creative

CONTINUED ON NEXT PAGE ☞

Other words: _____

_____

Write each word you circled and give a brief example that proves it describes you.

1. _____

_____

_____

2. _____

_____

_____

3. _____

_____

_____

4. _____

_____

_____

5. _____

_____

_____

CONTINUED ON NEXT PAGE ☞

Part II: Knowledge

Knowledge skills, as they relate to teaching, are bodies of technical information you have acquired about a particular subject or instructional technique.

Circle five or more phrases that represent your strongest knowledge skills.

Administrative Work

Working with IEPs
Setting up modular, flexible scheduling
Establishing accurate assessment systems
Prioritizing needed changes
Overseeing new program development
Other: _____

Student Motivation/Discipline

Implementing contract learning
Implementing effective discipline programs
Resolving conflicts
Using peer tutors
Motivating students
Counseling students
Other: _____

Instruction/Curriculum

Teaching with computers
Establishing and managing classroom
    learning-centers
Using cooperative learning approaches
Designing developmentally appropriate
    instruction
Incorporating whole language concepts into
    curricula
Implementing research on learning styles
Working with gifted students
Working with special needs students
Working with bilingual students

Working with nonEnglish-speaking students
Teaching critical thinking skills
Applying a multicultural perspective to
    curricula
Creating instructional materials
Adapting or developing curriculum
    guidelines
Other: _____

Experiences with Other Professionals and Parents

Teaching or planning within teams
Mentoring
Effectively communicating with parents
Actively involving parents
Using community resources
Inservice training

Extracurricular Activities

Supervising a classroom or school newspaper
Directing school plays
Conducting education research
Leading workshops
Organizing fund-raising efforts
Writing/publishing books, articles, etc.
Initiating public relations campaigns
Others: _____

CONTINUED ON NEXT PAGE ☞

On the lines below, write each phrase you circled and two or three sentences that elaborate on your expertise in this area.

1. _____

   _____

   _____

2. _____

   _____

   _____

3. _____

   _____

   _____

4. _____

   _____

   _____

5. _____

   _____

   _____

CONTINUED ON NEXT PAGE ☛

Part III: Abilities

Abilities, also known as transferrable skills, are skills you have that transfer to occupations outside of school. These skills tend to come automatically for you, like organizing, managing, writing, or working with your hands. They show potential supervisors that you have skills you can apply to new areas related to teaching. For example, the writing skills you use to publish your church newsletter could enable you to participate in the new emphasis on whole language in the school curriculum.

Which of the words below apply to you? Circle three to five that you have consistently undertaken. Think in terms of the moments in your life when you felt a sense of accomplishment or pride. Think in terms of compliments you have received or times when you were asked to help or train others.

Influenced	Persuaded	Promoted	Established	Advised	Directed
Counseled	Arranged	Wrote	Revised	Adapted	Coordinated
Managed	Expanded	Hired	Planned	Improved	Scheduled
Strengthened	Coached	Clarified	Simplified	Promoted	Negotiated

Other words:_____

For each word you circled, write the word and give a brief example that supports your claim to it.

1. _____

_____

2. _____

_____

3. _____

_____

4. _____

_____

5. _____

_____

Select Your Top Five Strengths

Review the words and phrases you circled in the previous exercises. From that group, select the five items you believe reflect your top skills. If possible, choose at least one item from each of the three skill categories: Qualities, Knowledge, and Abilities.

1. _____

2. _____

3. _____

4. _____

5. _____

Reword these five items a bit so they are grammatically uniform (i.e. all nouns or descriptive phrases) and their meanings are immediately clear.

1. _____

2. _____

3. _____

4. _____

5. _____

Prove Your Strengths

You've identified your top five work strengths. Now it's time to support those claims with hardcore evidence. At this point, the more details you can summon from the past, the better your case. Use the checklist at right to help you write three or four descriptive paragraphs about each of your top work strengths.

Below is a sample exercise:

In 1989, 45 percent of the special education students at Sandy High School in Westbend, Connecticut, could not pass driver's education. Under the guidance of the driver's education teacher, I adapted the instructional materials. I reworded worksheets, simplified assignments, and instituted a peer-tutoring program in which students with driver's licenses coached special education students on driving rules and regulations.

Sandy High School is the largest school in Connecticut, with more than five special education programs and where providing effective special-education programs is a top priority.

To date, 235 of its special education students have completed the driver's ed curricula I adapted. Of these, 80 percent have passed the state's written and behind-the-wheel driver's tests. The course continues to fill up each semester.

As a result of this success, I was asked to chair the school's curriculum committee.

Description Checklist

For each work strength you describe:

1. **Specify a significant achievement that required you to use this strength.**
   Describe the achievement in general. Then list specific tasks and responsibilities you performed to reach the ultimate outcome.

2. **Tell when you exhibited this achievement.**
   Describe the specific time period or frequency.

3. **Describe where you exhibited this achievement**
   List the place, the size of the place, and its reputation. If reputation is difficult to describe, then describe the expectations or the atmosphere of the place.

4. **Describe how well you exhibited the achievement.**
   Did someone or some group give you an award or point out your work to others? Were you asked to do it again or to use it somewhere else? Can you list measurable outcomes or enduring effects of the achievement?

CONTINUED ON NEXT PAGE ☞

STRENGTH #1: _____

_____

_____

_____

_____

_____

_____

_____

STRENGTH #2: _____

_____

_____

_____

_____

_____

_____

_____

_____

CONTINUED ON NEXT PAGE ☛

Prove Your Strengths (continued)

STRENGTH #3: _____

_____

_____

_____

_____

_____

_____

STRENGTH #4 : _____

_____

_____

_____

_____

_____

_____

_____

_____

CONTINUED ON NEXT PAGE ☞

STRENGTH #5 : _____

_____

_____

_____

_____

_____

_____

_____

Write a Work-Strengths Summary

A *work-strengths summary* is a concise summary of your teaching strengths. Composing such a document will help you summarize what you have learned about yourself, and it can serve as a handy reference when you are discussing your skills with a job contact. It is not a formal resume. It simply lists your major job skills and accomplishments.

Anatomy of a Work Strengths Summary

Work-strengths summaries have three basic sections:

1. *Personal Data*: The top of the first page lists your name, your address, and a phone number where a potential employer may leave you a message.
2. *Job Strengths*: The next section describes your top strengths, and achievements related to those strengths. Each strength should be no longer than two paragraphs. (In other words, use a shortened version of the strengths you just described on the previous pages.)
3. *Job Experience*. The remaining portion briefly summarizes your teaching and/or related work experience in chronological order, from most current to least current.

Activity

Use the work-strengths summary on the next two pages as a model for typing a summary of your own work strengths. Once you've completed your summary, ask people who know you well if they think it describes your abilities. Do they think you left anything out? What would they change?

Then rewrite, rewrite, rewrite, until your work-strengths summary conveys to others what you do best.

IAN HUNTER'S WORK-STRENGTHS SUMMARY

Ian Hunter

411 Alexander Street
Columbia, MO 65120
314-443-5960
(home and message phone)

WORK STRENGTHS

Curriculum Adaptation

Made Special Students Successful in Driver's Education

At Sandy High School, in Westbend, Connecticut, 45 percent of the special education students could not pass driver's education. Working with the driver's ed teacher, I adapted worksheets and assignments and established an effective peer-tutoring program. Eighty percent of special education students now pass the course. Of these, 90 percent go on to pass their state driver's test. As a result of this effort, the principal has appointed me to the school's curriculum committee.

Vocational Development

Helped Special Students Find Jobs

At Thomas High School in Columbia, Missouri, I set up a job course to help students referred from special education classes and the diversified occupations class to find after-school jobs. Seventy percent of those who completed the course found employment.

Computer Training and Implementation

Helped Students and Teachers Make Good Use of Computers

At Thomas High School, I trained special education students to use Macintosh computers to publish their own newsletter. I also provided support service to teachers who were interested in teaching with Macintosh computers, and I set up a system on the computers to track IEPs and class scheduling. This system is still being used five years later.

Mentoring

Mentored Three Beginning Teachers

During the last six years, I have served as a teacher mentor to three beginning teachers interested in teaching at-risk children or children with special needs. I provided them with advice and support in these areas: instruction, student management, scheduling and planning, and working with parents. All three enjoy fulfilling teaching positions to this day.

Public Speaking

Conducted Workshops on Vocational Training

For the past 10 years, I have conducted workshops for teachers and local agencies on vocational training and how it relates to dropout prevention. Clients include: Parrot Creek Boys Ranch, Project WAGE, and the Connecticut State Teachers Association.

JOB EXPERIENCE

1988-present

Special Educator; taught high school language arts and vocational studies to special education students.
Sandy High School, Westbend, Connecticut

1973-1988

Special Educator; taught high school English, social studies, and health to special education students.
Thomas High School, Columbia, Missouri

Visualize Your New Job

Executive placement consultants advise job seekers to use work-strengths summaries in a visualization exercise that can help them remain focused on their job-search goals. A mind focused on a goal, they claim, is like a powerful magnet that attracts the success it seeks.

Here is how the visualization exercise works:

Picture This:

Every morning and every evening of your job search, take out your summary and read it. Visualize yourself at your new job, using the skills written in your summary. Visualize the details of your new classroom, your co-workers, your parking space, the faculty room, your students and their parents. Each day, visualize a different teaching event or task. As you learn more about the school districts you would like to work in, visualize the school in greater detail.

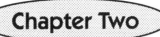
Chapter Two

SURVEY PROSPECTIVE SCHOOLS

You began your job search by carefully assessing yourself—your career goals and work strengths. Your next step is to compile a list of schools that interest you and to uncover enough information about those schools that you can carefully assess them as well.

If the goals and strengths of some of these schools are compatible with the personal ones you outlined in the previous chapter, then you will know where to target your job-search energies.

If, on the other hand, your investigations lead you to delete more than a comfortable number of schools from your list, then continue the search with yet another round of schools.

The best way to gather information about specific schools is to consult with a number of people who are directly or indirectly associated with the schools. I call these consultations *school surveys*.

A school survey is like a job interview in reverse. *You* ask the questions and evaluate the answers. This chapter will help you locate potential consultants or advisers, set up appointments with them, devise a list of useful questions to ask them, and evaluate the answers they give you.

Network Your Way to a List of Schools

On a separate sheet of paper, jot down the names of schools where you would like to teach. Also list the names of cities, towns, or counties where you would like to teach, but are unfamiliar with the schools.

You'll need to do a little networking to locate the names of good schools that operate in the cities, towns, and counties you mentioned. That means making some phone calls to people who are familiar with the schools in those areas. You don't have to know these people by name. You just need a phone book and a little determination. Call employees of the local Chamber of Commerce, regional school suppliers, or area realtors and ask them to recommend good schools.

Steps to Effective Networking

Following are four steps you can use to solicit recommendations effectively. Study the model, but don't copy it word for word. Develop your own approach so that it sounds natural for you. Practice it a few times on yourself and a friend. Then go out and network!

1. Tell why you are asking the person for advice.
   - *(To school supplier)* "You service schools in this area . . ."
   - *(To realtor, Chamber of Commerce member)* "You know this town, I thought you might . . ."
   - *(To organization head)* "You work with teachers and schools in the area of . . ."

- *(To state official)* "You fund school grants in the area of . . ."

2. Ask for advice, not jobs.
   - "Can you recommend a school that has an excellent reputation?"

3. Describe any specific types of information you are looking for.
   - "I'm looking for an opportunity to teach:
     - mildly handicapped high school students.
     - vocational education.
     - early childhood classes."

4. Thank the person and request an opportunity to check back.
   - "May I check back with you later for more ideas?"

Ranking Your List

After you have completed your networking, rank your schools from most desirable to least desirable. If this is difficult to determine, give top priority to those schools that were:

- recommended by the people you trust most,
- described as schools that emphasized your interests, and/or
- mentioned by more than one person.

Search for Potential Advisers

Sorry, there is no "best people in teaching" list. To determine who to talk with at length about the schools of your choice, begin by compiling lists of people who have a working relationship with your prospective schools. If you can identify these sources by name, do so. If not, write down general job titles, and then go back and use your networking skills to get the names.

The most obvious people to serve as advisers—classroom teachers, school-board members, and local college faculty—are the ones most often used by everybody else. You want to talk with these traditional sources, but you also want to brainstorm for some creative sources.

Brainstorming for Sources

Look at the chart below to help you get started. In the left-hand column, under Job Site and General Experts, are the traditional sources of information. As you move from left to right, less obvious sources appear. First there's the Local People in Related Services column; then there's the Local Sales and Service Community column.

Your Own Chart

Make your own chart of potential advisers on a separate sheet of paper. Consider all sources valid. Some of your best information will come from sources that you see once a year or less. In job hunting, this is known as the strength of weak ties. In one study, those job seekers who networked with people they met once a year or less found jobs that paid $2,500 a year more than those job seekers who concentrated on asking family, friends, and colleagues.

Potential Advisers for School Surveys

Job Site and General Experts

- Classroom teachers
- Guidance counselors
- Managers of local college placement offices
- Managers of the district's personnel offices
- School administrators
- School-board members
- Faculty at local colleges of education
- Officials at the state department of education
- Statewide education specialists

Local People in Related Services

- PTA/PTO officers
- Teachers' union officials
- Consultants in fields of special interest to you, such as computers or process writing

Local Sales and Service Community

- Textbook salespeople
- Newspaper reporters
- Librarians
- Directors of recreational programs
- Town council members

Develop a List of Questions For Advisers

What types of questions should you ask your advisers in order to get the best information possible about prospective schools?

Ask about the school's philosophy, management styles, and working conditions; about improvements the school could use; about education trends and changes that might affect the school; and for career and job-search advice.

Below are sample questions. Some are appropriate for laypeople, such as reporters, PTA officials, or secretaries. Others are questions for experts, such as teachers, administrators, or state-agency personnel.

Start a notebook and put these titles on three separate pages: Questions to Ask Experts, Questions to Ask People in Related Fields, and Questions to Ask Others (Sales and Community Service). Later, you may wish to add a fourth page: Questions to Ask at Interviews. For now, jot down appropriate questions on each of the three pages. Use some of the sample questions below as well as your own.

Philosophy, Management Styles, And Working Conditions

- What does the district, school, or department do best?
- Why do you like working here?
- Why do you like working in this community?
- What is the general discipline policy or emphasis?
- What are the expectations for teachers by their supervisors?
- How are people evaluated?
- What are the annual goals for this school?
- Are teachers' opinions solicited about future changes?
- What are the strengths of the current staff?
- What does it take to enjoy working here?

- What are typical classroom budgets like?
- What is the student-teacher ratio?
- Who are some of the top people?
- What makes them special?
- Are there any articles, brochures, or policy statements I might read?
- May I tour your school sometime?

Unmet Needs

- If you could change anything about the school what would it be?
- What improvements would you like to see funded?
- What are some parental concerns?
- What students could use more services?
- What types of services?
- What types of skills would help make the staff more complete?

Trends and Changes

- How have you seen the school change in the last few years?
- Are there any new laws or regulations that will impact this school?
- What type of staff development is being planned?
- Is the school implementing any new trends in the testing or grouping of students?
- Are there any staffing changes being contemplated?
- Are there any new education studies you would recommend I read?
- Are there any new techniques/methods you would recommend I investigate?

Career Advice

- What are some pitfalls new teachers/staffers typically face here?
- Who helped you the most when you first came to this school?
- What is the district currently looking for in new teachers /staffers?
- What type of teacher/staffer stays a long time at this school?
- Why?
- What makes someone successful in this school?
- Looking at my work-strengths summary, how would you think I might fit in here?
- Which of my experiences need to be more fully described?
- Which of my experiences would you minimize or delete?
- Do you see any areas I am weak in?
- What areas would be an asset?

Job Search Advice

- When are most jobs advertised?
- Are jobs filled throughout the year?
- Are substitutes ever hired full time?
- What type of substitute makes a good impression here?
- How can I best prepare for an interview at this school?
- Is there a pre-employment interview?
- What should I know before going into a job interview at this school?
- Can you recommend two other people I might talk to?

Set Up Appointments for School Surveys

Now it's time to arrange appointments for your school surveys. This is about the time many job seekers start to get cold feet. Sure, school surveys sound like a great idea, they say, but will busy and important people really want to talk with me? Guess what! Most people love to talk about themselves and what they do. If you contact one of the few who is reluctant, just ask him or her to recommend someone else who might be more available.

Phone vs. Letter

A phone call is usually the quickest way to set up a personal meeting. Be prepared, however, to make more than one call if you are trying to reach a busy person.

If you feel more comfortable initiating this appointment with a letter, that's fine. But keep in mind that in most cases a letter will still require verification by phone.

Make sure your phone or letter request covers the following:

- The types of information you are looking for (refer to previous question-writing exercise)
- How much time you would like (about 25 minutes)
- A convenient time to meet (before, after, or during the work day)

I suggest that you make your first appointments with advisers from schools that you placed at the bottom of your list. That way, if you make any startup mistakes, your flaws will be inconsequential.

Whenever possible, talk with at least three persons associated with a school of interest. Start with the person least directly associated with the school (such as a town council member) and gradually progress toward the ones with the most direct involvement. That way, by the time you talk with someone with hiring power, you will have learned a lot about the school. You will sound knowledgeable about it and committed to its mission.

Referrals

Should you use a referral's name when you call for an appointment? First, ask the person who gave you the tip: "Do you mind if I mention your name when I contact Mr. Wonderful?" If your contact hesitates, quickly indicate that you will not use his or her name.

Second, only mention your referral if you have good reason to believe Mr. Wonderful likes him or her. You can't always determine this, but usually, if the referral has mostly positive things to say about Mr. Wonderful, then Mr. Wonderful probably views your referral in a positive manner as well.

One More Sticky Question

Some of the people you contact will ask you if you are job seeking. Be honest. If you are looking, say, "Yes, I am looking for a future job, and I want to talk to some of the best people in the field in order to get a jump on future openings." Or, you can say, "I will be applying in the future. Right now, I am surveying schools to learn which districts/schools have goals and teaching styles similar to my own."

Make the Most of School Surveys

Before you embark upon your first school surveys, I would like to remind you that your advisers will be left with a very definite impression of you based upon the quality of your appearance and discussion. The following is my advice on making the most of those qualities.

Appearance

When setting out for a school survey, dress equal to or slightly more formal than the person you are going to meet. If you are unsure of what to wear, call a school secretary and ask about typical school dress.

Speaking of appearance, make sure you appear on time. When you are making an appointment, always get specific directions to your the meeting place.

Discussion

Take your list of questions and your work-strengths summary to each meeting. These papers should keep the conversation flowing. Remember, too, that a school survey is a job interview in reverse—your purpose is to ask the questions and privately evaluate the answers. That means that your adviser should do most of the talking.

Never Stretch the Purpose of a School Survey

Conducting school surveys is a wonderful way to investigate schools and teaching positions. However, you must never use this method as a ploy to get interviews and job offers. That would be abusing your advisers' generosity. You told them you were gathering information to make better application choices—and that's the way it should stay. Stretching the purpose of the school survey can also get you in trouble with personnel departments if they find out you are trying to go around their hiring processes.

There are many ways to clarify the purpose of school surveys, should it be necessary.

First, if someone asks you to bring a resume—don't. Instead say, "I don't have a resume at this point. Right now, I just want to get some advice and learn about your school. But, when I do apply, I will be happy to send you one."

You could take your work-strengths summary to the school survey instead and get it evaluated. Ask the person you meet with to evaluate the strengths you listed on your summary and indicate the ones that would be of greatest interest to the school. You'll learn in the process what the district wants and what you don't yet have. This advice might also cause you to remember something you forgot to include in the summary.

Second, if you are offered a job (as I have been) at the end of a school survey, again, clarify your intention. Simply tell the consultant how flattered you are to hear the offer. However, re-affirm that you are still thinking and looking and will let him or her know as soon as you have completed your information gathering and can make a decision. This is professional, and it can increase your value later if you decide to apply formally. Employers may be prepared to negotiate conditions, such as classrooms, student count, or experience-salary issues when you are desired, but not yet available. It is hard to turn down the offer, but you owe it to yourself and the job seekers who will come after you to preserve the integrity of the school survey.

Survey Your Surveys

How do you know if your school surveys were successful? What do you do with the mounds of advice you accumulated? The following guidelines will help you appraise the results of your school surveys.

Evaluating School Surveys

Use these three criteria to determine if a session was successful:
- You talked only 10 to 20 percent of the time.
- You kept to your allotted time.
- You felt good about your abilities and potential after leaving.

Summarizing Information

You will sometimes find it difficult to keep track of all the names, places, and advice you encounter. Keep a file on each school you are serious about. In each folder, store notes, pamphlets, and thoughts about the school. Try to answer these questions on a sheet in each folder:
- How do my skills and interests fit this school?
- What is this district/school proud of?
- What are some unmet needs I could assist in?
- What would be some of my weaknesses in the eyes of this school, and how can I plan to strengthen them?

Verifying Advice

In general, the advice you gather from your school surveys will be extremely valuable. But this does not mean that all of it is accurate or that you should always follow it. Before you act on any advice, such as taking a course or rewriting your resume, verify the advice with another opinion.

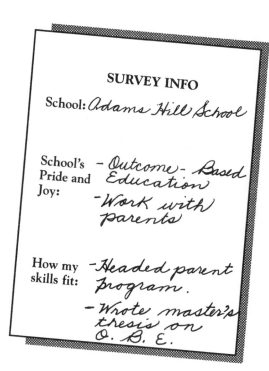

SURVEY INFO

School: *Adams Hill School*

School's Pride and Joy: - Outcome - Based Education - Work with parents

How my skills fit: - Headed parent program. - Wrote master's thesis on O. B. E.

Write Thank-You Notes

Every adviser who spends time helping you deserves your thanks. While you're reviewing your surveys, jot down the names of each adviser. Send each one on your list a typed or handwritten note that acknowledges their help.

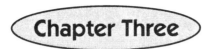

Chapter Three

WRITE THE RIGHT RESUME

Now that you have determined which schools or school districts you would like to pursue, you are ready to write a resume.

Most employers require you to submit a resume before they will consider you for an official job interview.

A *resume* concisely and convincingly summarizes your interests, strengths, and work-related experiences in an organized format.

A truly effective resume also sells you. It catches employers' attention by giving them a quick snapshot of you as a unique and interesting person with—here's the most important part—work potential that is consistent with their needs. It makes you stand out from the resume pile.

A resume is only one tool in your job search. But it can be a crucial one. It can make or break your opportunity for a job interview. Usually it takes less than a minute for a potential employer to scan your resume and decide whether or not to grant you an interview. This is particularly true if the employer doesn't know anything about you. At this point, a well-written resume is your only ally.

Now, if you've done your networking, an employer may already have an inkling of who you are. In this case, a well-written resume strengthens that image and further increases your chances for an interview.

The following chapter shows how to project your personal best into a resume that also targets the needs of a specific employer. It helps you write the right resume to get your foot in the school door of your choice.

ARE YOU READY TO WRITE A GREAT RESUME?

Take this quiz to find out if you are truly ready to write a great resume. For each question, circle "True" or "False."

1. Employers want to see job responsibilities, not accomplishments, in a resume.

   True   False

2. It should take you about three hours to write a resume.

   True   False

3. You should limit your resume to one page.

   True   False

4. You should always put "References available upon request" at the bottom of your resume.

   True   False

5. You should always use complete sentences in your resume.

   True   False

6. During a job search, you may need to write several different resumes.

   True   False

7. It's alright to exaggerate your job responsibilities a bit. After all, you are trying to sell yourself.

   True   False

8. It's not a good idea to go into detail about volunteer work or community activities.

   True   False

Answers to Quiz:

1. *False.* Employers want both types of information. For each job they want to know your specific responsibilities, and then they want to know what you accomplished with those responsibilities.

2. *False.* If you begin with the self-assessment and goal-setting exercises in Chapter 1, use that information to develop a work-strengths summary like the one in the first chapter, compare your work strengths with those of schools you investigated in Chapter 2, and then write your resume, it will take five to 15 hours. You can also expect to write several drafts before you finalize your resume. Hard work, you say? Absolutely. But a well-written resume signals employers that you are a hard and thorough worker.

   The best way to go about the writing and rewriting is to do a little bit of the task every few days over a period of several weeks. Don't do it all at once. Like wine maturing in a cellar, good ideas will ripen and come to you. Tackle the project about one to five hours per week. Never do more than two hours at one sitting.

3. *False.* You can't always summarize 20 years of work experience in one, or even two, pages. Take whatever you need to tell your story—but do it as succinctly as possible.

4. *False.* It is not inappropriate, but it is certainly unnecessary to list "References available upon request" at the end of your resume. Most potential employers assume that if they request references after your interview, you will comply.

   Whatever you do, never list specific references on your resume. You don't want anyone who isn't strongly considering you to call your references and consume their valuable time.

5. *False.* Use sentence fragments instead of complete sentences. They are faster to read, take up less space, and often force you to be concise.

6. *True.* You don't need a new resume for every new interview. But, you always need a resume that's relevant to the type of job you are pursuing. In some cases, that may require you to tailor the job-objective statement and job experiences on your standard resume to fit those of a specific job opening.

7. *False.* Never alter a job title or inflate job responsibilities. At some point, your background may be checked or you will be asked to elaborate. Stick with emphasizing your strengths.

8. *False.* If your volunteer work or community service demonstrates important work strengths or teaching skills, by all means, give details.

Scoring:

Did you miss less than two answers? Congratulations, you are among the resume literate! I still suggest you review the material in this chapter before you finalize your resume. You may pick up a few new ideas.

If you missed more than two questions, you'll find this chapter very helpful in developing an effective resume.

SPELL CHECK!

QUESTION: Is it resume, résumé, or résume?

ANSWER: It's up to you! Webster's says all three are correct, but it gives preference to spelling it with two accent marks, then with one mark, and then with none. If you are an English teacher, you might want to use Webster's first preference, if for no other reason than to show prospective employers you know your Webster's.

On the other hand, the writers and editors of most job-search books believe the accent marks are distracting to readers. Some use one accent to differentiate between the verb *resume* (to continue) and the noun *resume* (as in summary sheet), but the majority use no accent marks. In this book, I've decided to follow the crowd.

WHAT'S YOUR RESUME STYLE?

There are two main types of resume styles to choose from: *chronological* and *functional*. Each style provides the same general information—personal data, job objective(s), work experience, work skills and accomplishments, and education. It just does it in a different way. Neither style is better. It depends upon your circumstances. Let's look at each style—its strengths and weaknesses, when it should and should not be used, and its basic format.

Chronological Resume

The *chronological resume* is used by more job seekers than the functional resume. It highlights employment experience in reverse chronological order, starting with the most recent job and going back in time.

In a chronological resume, you list each job title, its corresponding company/school, the dates you held the job, and a brief description of your duties and accomplishments.

Strengths

- More accepted
- Emphasizes job continuity and growth
- Easier to organize and write
- Easier to read

Weaknesses

- Calls attention to job gaps, lateral moves, and frequent or unrelated job changes
- Rigid format

When to Use

Use when your job history is straightforward and indicates growth and development.

When to Avoid

Avoid when you are a job hopper, when you have long gaps of unemployment that you wish to downplay, or when you have limited job experience.

SAMPLE CHRONOLOGICAL FORMAT

NAME
ADDRESS
TELEPHONE NUMBER

JOB OBJECTIVE

PROFESSIONAL EXPERIENCE

Job Title, Employer, Dates *(most recent)*
- Responsibility; accomplishment
- Responsibility; accomplishment
- Responsibility: accomplishment

Job Title, Employer, Dates
- Responsibility; accomplishment
- Responsibility; accomplishment
- Responsibility: accomplishment

Job Title, Employer, Dates
- Responsibility; accomplishment
- Responsibility; accomplishment
- Responsibility: accomplishment

PROFESSIONAL ACTIVITIES

COMMUNITY SERVICE *(if relevant)*

EDUCATION

Institution, Degree, Year Issued *(optional)*

Functional Resume

A *functional resume* focuses on skills and accomplishments. It uses skills instead of job titles as headings. Under each skill heading are related job responsibilities and accomplishments.

Strengths

- Emphasizes skills and accomplishments
- Downplays career gaps
- Flexible
- Can be very creative
- Can be more readily organized in the order you want employer to read

Weaknesses

- More difficult to organize and write
- More difficult to read

When to Use

Use when you are entering the job market for the first time, when you are re-entering the market after a gap of any length, when you have gaps of unemployment you wish to downplay, when you wish to change careers, or when you've had many unrelated jobs.

When to Avoid

Avoid when you wish to emphasize job stability or the schools or companies with which you have been affiliated.

SAMPLE FUNCTIONAL FORMAT

NAME
ADDRESS
TELEPHONE NUMBER

JOB OBJECTIVE

SKILLS
Skill *(most important)*
- Responsibility; accomplishment
- Responsibility; accomplishment
- Responsibility; accomplishment

Skill
- Responsibility; accomplishment
- Responsibility; accomplishment
- Responsibility; accomplishment

Skill
- Responsibility; accomplishment
- Responsibility; accomplishment
- Responsibility; accomplishment

PROFESSIONAL EXPERIENCE
Job Title, Employer, Dates *(most recent)*
Job Title, Employer, Dates
Job Title, Employer, Dates

EDUCATION
Institution, Degree, Year Issued *(optional)*

READY, SET, WRITE!

By now you should have decided which of the two resume formats is right for you. No matter which one you have chosen, you can use the following instructions to create a master resume.

Later, as you apply for specific jobs, you may want to tailor your "master" to better show how your aspirations and experiences match the employer's expectations.

As far as design goes, I will give you general placement instructions, but I leave specific placement of information up to you. Do try to keep the design simple and easy to read. Double-space your lines and make your margins at least one inch on all sides to avoid a cramped look. When you have completed your resume, type it or print it out on white or off-white bond paper, using black ink. You know your design is successful if a reader can scan all key points within seconds.

1. Identification

At the very top of your resume, write your full name, followed by your home address (including zip code) and a telephone number where potential employers can contact you or leave you a message.

2. Job Objective

In five lines or less, tell what you are looking for in an education position. If you can do so without eliminating acceptable options, specify education level, type of student, type of school environment, subject areas, and school issues that interest you most.

If you need help determining a suitable objective, turn back to Chapter 1 and reread the answers you supplied in Exercise 1: Describe Your Ideal Job. Then look at the job objectives in the sample resumes at the end of this chapter.

It is not essential to provide a job objective on your resume, but it often can help. One way employers pare down a stack of resumes is to flip through the job objective sections and select ones that most closely match their needs.

3. Work Experiences/Skills

This is the heart of your resume. It is where you prove to potential employers that you are qualified to perform your job objective.

You have completed some of the preliminary thinking for this section already. You'll find it in the form of the Work-Strengths Summary you wrote (Chapter 1) and the file folders you created during your school investigations (Chapter 2). Take out these materials and refer to them as you complete the section.

If you are using a chronological format, read the instructions for the "Teaching Experience" section. If you have chosen a functional format, read the instructions for the "Skills" section.

For Teaching Experiences Section:

In reverse chronological order, list the time span and title of each teaching job you have held. Under each title, add the name and location of the school and a one-sentence description of the job. Under each description, list your major work responsibilities. Whenever possible, support these statements with related outcomes. For example:

1990-92: FIFTH GRADE LANGUAGE ARTS TEACHER
Lakeside Elementary School New Orleans, LA.

Responsible for teaching reading, grammar, composition, and spelling to 75 fifth grade students who are grouped into three mixed-ability classes.
• Instituted a whole-language reading program that resulted in a 15 percent increase in fifth grade students who tested above grade level in reading

- Used word-processing software and the process-writing approach to help fifth grade students develop better skills in writing, spelling, and grammar
- Produced three all-school plays that enjoyed sell-out crowds

As you write, keep your job objective and the objectives of your chosen schools in mind. Try to tailor your experiences to meet these objectives.

For Skills Section:

List three to five personal skills that relate to your job objective. Start with the skill most crucial to your job objective, follow with the next most crucial, and so on. Next to each declared skill, describe specific job responsibilities, accomplishments, and measurable outcomes that support your claim. For example:

> CURRICULUM ADAPTATION
> Established a peer-tutoring program and adapted textbook readings and assignments to help learning disabled (LD) students at Springfield High School in Rolla, Missouri, pass the sophomore biology requirement. The number of LD students that passed the course increased 40 percent after the initiation of this program.

For Both Sections:

Make sure that all of the statements you write in this section support your job objective. Emphasize the experiences that come the closest to the job you want. And whenever possible, use convincing examples and details.

Once you have written this section, go back and delete any redundant phrases or unnecessary words. Minimize the use of "I," and maximize the use of action words. Ensure that the writing conveys your personality and your enthusiasm for your work.

If your professional teaching experiences are limited, include the following types of experiences:
- Any work in schools. Include substitute teaching, practicum, student teaching, part-time, or full-time experiences.
- General work with young people. This can include work with agencies, camps, parent groups, community groups, and so on.
- Any experiences that reveal your maturity, responsibility, and people skills. These experiences can include parenting, jobs working with the public, or volunteer work.

4. Employment History

If you are writing a functional resume, include a brief employment history. Supply the job title, employer, and dates of employment only. Here's an example:

EMPLOYMENT HISTORY
1989-present: Fifth Grade Teacher
Rock Creek Elementary School, Washington, D.C.

1985-89: Social Worker
City Youth Council, Washington, D.C.

5. Education

For each degree you have earned, list the type of degree, the school you received it from, the year you received the degree, your major, and any teaching certification or honors that were granted to you.

(Note: You may want to designate a separate section for credentials only. These may include administrative internship credentials, multiple or specific subject certifications, and certificates of competence.

6. Personal Information, Activities, and Statements (Optional)

Some job seekers end their resume with a list of additional interests or skills (such as foreign language fluency or computer literacy). Some list their memberships in professional organizations. Still others list awards they have received or community service work they have performed. All of this information is optional, but if you think any of it reveals positive personality traits or if it underscores your interest and expertise in education, by all means, use it!

You could also end with a brief summary of your deepest motivation or reason for teaching.

One special educator I know ended a resume by pointing out that all of her life she has worked with physically disadvantaged people. (She grew up with a physically disadvantaged brother, so this was certainly true.)

A recent college graduate I know ended with a long-term goal statement about the contribution he hopes to make to the field: "My master teacher described my work as 'detailed, diligent, and thoroughly organized.' I hope to build upon these qualities in my next job."

7. References

Do not include a reference section in which you list the names of persons who can speak on your behalf. They are busy people. You want to ensure that only employers who are seriously considering you will take up their valuable time. Employers who are serious about you will ask for references if they need them.

Although it is not inappropriate to tack "References available upon request," at the end of your resume, there's no need to use up good space doing it. Most employers assume that if they need references from you, you will comply.

TIP:

After you have completed your master resume, cover the job statement and ask someone to guess what it is by reading the remainder of the resume. If your reader is incorrect or is confused about the objective, ask why. (It's usually because you have included experiences that detract from your main purpose.)

EVALUATE AND REWRITE

You are not done yet! Now it is time to evaluate your efforts. I recommend you do this on three levels.

Level One: Self-Evaluation

First, evaluate the piece yourself. Cover up your goal and ask yourself: "What type of job does this resume suggest I am looking for? Do all my Work Experience or Skills statements support this objective? Did I provide enough examples and details to back up these statements? Did I minimize the use of jargon, acronyms, and abbreviations?"

Level Two: Evaluation by A Friend or Co-Worker

Next, go to someone who knows your work or training experience. Ask that person the same types of questions. For example: "Is my resume clear? What parts seem confusing? What parts are most convincing? Do the experiences support my goal? Did I overlook any important skills or experiences? Did I include any information that you think I should shorten or delete? Are there statements that need more explanation? Are the format and sequence of the resume clear?"

Level Three: Evaluation by Someone Who Makes Hiring Decisions

Now approach someone involved in hiring decisions (preferably in the field of education) who does not know you. This could be a personnel officer, a college-placement counselor, or even a school principal. Show the person the resume and ask him or her, "Compared to other resumes you have seen for the position of xyz, how would you say my experiences and resume format compare? Could you give me some honest feedback on the strengths and weaknesses?"

Use the feedback from these three evaluations to refine the first draft of your resume.

One Last Edit

You are still not done! Now it is time to edit your resume for brevity, clarity, consistent design, correct spelling, and correct and consistent grammar. Once you're done with that, give copies of your resume to three other persons and ask them to do the same. Then use this feedback to refine one last time.

RESUME EVALUATION CHECKLIST

Is your resume ready for the tough scrutiny of a potential employer? It is if you can check each of the following qualifications.

- ❑ All of my resume statements support my job objective.

- ❑ The organization of my experiences is immediately obvious and meaningful. The reader can scan all key points within seconds.

- ❑ I described all of my experiences with convincing examples or details.

- ❑ I emphasized all of my most important experiences—the experiences closest to the job I want.

- ❑ I did not repeat the same experiences in different parts of the resume.

- ❑ I have conveyed my personality and individual strengths and interests.

- ❑ My enthusiasm for what I want to do shines through.

- ❑ I deleted all unnecessary words. The word "I" does not appear too often. Action words begin sentences when possible.

- ❑ In order to avoid looking cramped, the design of my resume incorporates lots of white space. My margins are at least one inch on all sides. There is extra white space between major skill or experience areas.

- ❑ I capitalized, underlined, or typed important headings and subheadings in bold letters.

- ❑ My grammar is correct and consistently applied (for example, periods and capital letters are used the same way throughout).

- ❑ Wherever possible, I avoided jargon, acronyms, and abbreviations.

- ❑ My resume is printed on white or off-white bond paper with black ink.

- ❑ Three other people read my resume for clarity, correct grammar, and correct spelling.

CHRONOLOGICAL RESUME EXPERIENCED ELEMENTARY/JUNIOR HIGH TEACHER

CAROLYN STOVER
123 Local Street
Santa Cruz, CA 95063
415-999-2211

JOB OBJECTIVE

Seeking a junior high school position where my interests in writing, literature, and drama can be fully used. Also interested in using creative activities to improve self-esteem in at-risk students.

TEACHING EXPERIENCES

1987-Present: Seventh and Eighth Grade Teacher (English for Low Achievers)
John Hall Junior High School, Santa Cruz, CA

Teach a creative writing program for low achievers that incorporates pre-writing, student–teacher conferences, guest speakers, editing, revising, and publishing.

- As part of the publishing segment of this program, students produce (via word processor) a monthly student journal. This is the first time most of these students have ever seen their writing published.
- Other teachers have recently sought my help in using word processors to publish their own student newsletters and journals. As a result, I am in the process of setting up a student publishing center in the school.
- Last year helped interested students write and produce their own play. The play was performed for parents during our Spring Program.

1984-87: Sixth Grade Classroom Teacher
Kennedy Elementary School, Santa Cruz, CA

Taught all major sixth grade subjects in a self-contained classroom.

- Incorporated whole language concepts into everyday math and science curricula.
- Collected literature for my own reading curriculum. Was asked to share list with the faculty.
- Helped produce the school's first student newspaper—*The Kennedy Observer*. It is still published today.

EDUCATION

1984: Bachelor of Science, Elementary Education, University of California at Santa Cruz. Elementary Education Certification.

OTHER ACTIVITIES

1990-91: Wrote a monthly column entitled "Writer's Corner" for *Today's Teacher* magazine.
Summer 1984-88: Directed Children's Summer Playhouse in Santa Cruz, CA.

CHRONOLOGICAL RESUME EXPERIENCED HIGH SCHOOL TEACHER

CHRISTOPHER SIEGEL

123 Local Street
Corvallis, OR 97330
503-999-2211

JOB OBJECTIVE

Interested in a high school teaching position in which I can investigate ways of linking science education with learning styles.

TEACHING EXPERIENCE

1988-Present: Biology Teacher
Corvallis High School, Corvallis, Oregon

Responsible for an integrated class of special and regular students.

- This year, recruited seniors from college prep classes to serve as peer tutors for the special education students. As a result, more of the special education students passed the course than in the previous years
- As part of the curriculum, all students use computerized self-paced anatomy lessons that I created myself.
- Am in the process of adapting those lessons to meet the needs of different learning modalities.

1979-88: Biology, Physics, and Computer Teacher
Crescent Valley High School, Eugene, Oregon

Taught classes in physics, biology, and computers.

- Designed plan for teaching physics with computers. Crescent Valley teachers still follow the plan today.
- Assisted junior varsity wrestling coach. Sent two students to state play-offs in 1988.

EDUCATION

1977: Bachelor of Arts, Biology, San Francisco State University, California.
1979: Oregon Basic Secondary Teaching Certificate. Oregon State University, Corvallis, OR.

OTHER ACTIVITIES

Summer 1990: Oceanography Self-Study
Travelled up and down the West Coast studying tide pools and estuaries. Kept detailed sketches that appeared in the April 1991 issue of *California* magazine.

1985-88: Environmental Newsletter
Helped publish a monthly tourist newsletter on coastal towns in Oregon.

FUNCTIONAL RESUME NEW TEACHER

WILLIAM FREDRICKS
123 Local Street, St. Louis, MO 63032
314-999-2211

JOB OBJECTIVE

Seeking elementary or high school teaching position in music (general, choral, orchestra, and/or band).
Would like to locate in Thurston County.

SKILLS

Teaching
- Student taught general music to all grades levels (K–6) at Martin Luther King, Jr. Elementary School, St. Louis, MO.
- Coordinated choral arts program, grades 9–12 at Thurston County Parks Recreation Center, Florrisant, MO, last summer. Two students became finalists in regional contests.

Directing and Producing
- Directed People First Choir at First Baptist Church, St. Louis, MO. for two years.
- Helped music teacher produce first Christmas musical at Martin Luther King Elementary School this year. It was well received by faculty, parents, and students.

Music
- Sing; play piano, guitar, and violin; compose and arrange.
- Received four-year music scholarship to University of St. Louis, MO.

WORK HISTORY

Piano Accompanist, First Baptist Church, St. Louis, MO; 1989-93

EDUCATION

Bachelor of Science, Music Emphasis, University of St. Louis in Missouri. Missouri; 1993
Continuing Teaching Certificate (K-12).

OTHER ACTIVITIES

Member, University of St. Louis Chamber Choir; 1991-92
Member, University of St. Louis Opera Association; 1990-92

FUNCTIONAL RESUME CAREER CHANGER

MONICA ORLANDO

6705 St. John's Landing
Santa Cruz, CA 95134
415-482-2122

JOB OBJECTIVE
Seeking a position as a school-site administrator.

SKILLS

Administrative
- Established language-development training program for the teaching staff of the Carmel School District in California. The program is in its fourth year.
- Organized a Teacher Forum on bilingual education for Carmel teachers. More than 50% of the faculty participated.
- Initiated process-writing program at three Carmel schools. Writing scores in these three schools increased 20% after the first year of the program's initiation.
- Administered staff training series on language acquisition, sheltered English, program quality review, and assertive discipline. Teachers reported that the training helped them better integrate new students and reduce classroom conflicts.

Teaching
- Taught Spanish language arts.
- Taught sixth and seventh grade social studies. Was lead social studies teacher for three years.

Spanish Fluency
- Taught Spanish language arts.
- Conducted after-school Spanish lessons for Carmel teaching staff.
- Taught physical education to Spanish-speaking children in Bolivia.

WORK HISTORY

Education Programs Specialist, Carmel School District, Carmel, CA; 1985 to present
Spanish and Social Studies Teacher, Wilson Junior High School, Carmel, CA; 1978-84
Teen Program Administrator, YMCA, San Mateo, CA; 1975-78
Instructor of Environmental Studies, University Extension, University of California, Santa Cruz, CA; 1973-74
Peace Corps Volunteer, Physical Education Teacher, Bolivia; 1970-72

EDUCATION

Master of Arts, Educational Administration, San Jose State University, San Jose, CA; 1992
Bachelor of Arts, (cum laude), Physical Education and Recreation, University of Southern California,
     Los Angeles, CA; 1970

CREDENTIALS

- Administrative Internship Credential California Multiple Subject Certification (K-9)
- California Bilingual Certificate of Competence (Spanish)

Chapter Four

LINE UP YOUR
INTERVIEWS

Now it is time to take all you have learned about yourself and the districts you wish to apply to and put this information to work. Your mission is to line up some serious job interviews. You will continue to gather information as you did before. However, now you will also file job applications, make direct contact with hiring authorities, mail placement files, and do any type of written or phone follow-up that can help you set up interview appointments.

FOLLOW THE FORMAL STEPS

Once you feel you have gathered all the information you need about a school or district of interest, call the central office and ask about current openings and how the district would like you to apply for them.

The formal steps usually include submitting an official application form along with a resume and a cover letter.

If a district has no current job openings, I still suggest you complete the formal application process to whatever extent possible. You never know when an opening will come along. Unexpected spouse transfers, medical leaves, and grant money can all provide sudden job openings. The farther along you are in the application process, the closer you are to securing that unforeseen job opportunity.

Application Form

Each school district has its own application form. The forms are similar in many respects, but the variations make it important to approach each one with a fresh eye. Also, the more you know about a specific district, the more you can tailor your responses to the specific curriculum and overall programs.

Below are some general pointers to keep in mind as you complete your application forms.

1. **Employers often reject applications based on the following errors:**
   - Messiness
   - Spelling and/or grammatical errors
   - Incomplete information
   - Information not typed or not handprinted (requirements vary from form to form)

   Ask a friend to check your completed forms for problems in any of these areas.

2.. **Make your responses brief and use action words whenever possible.** Action words make you sound energetic.

3. **Handle dates with care**. If some of your job experiences have been short-lived, round off your dates to the nearest month or year. If your dates betray your age and you feel that might be a problem, group your experience in general time frames. For example, instead of listing dates that indicate 15 or more years of experience, write "more than 12 years of experience."

4. **Avoid discussing any sensitive issue**. There is not enough room on most forms to support your case. For example: Suppose you had to leave a school district. When faced with an application question such as "Why did you leave the district?" leave it blank or write "Will discuss in person." This allows you to discuss the issue more fully and in its proper context.

Resume

Take out your master resume (the one you created by following the advice in Chapter 3) and read it carefully. Does it show how your special skills, strengths, and experiences meet the specific needs of the district you are applying to? If not, revise it accordingly.

Cover Letter

Along with your application form and targeted resume, you'll need to send a cover letter addressed to your prospective supervisor (get this person's name from personnel). The letter should describe your interest in securing a position in the district, provide a brief description of your job qualifications, and then actually ask for an interview. (See sample letter on next page.)

If the district is not conducting official interviews at this time, in place of a regular interview, ask for an exploratory interview in which you could discuss what you and the district might have to offer each other in the future.

SAMPLE COVER LETTER

Gene Farrell
109 Elm St.
Peoria, IL 61604

May 6, 1993

Dr. Paula Sanders
Bentley Junior High School
39 River Road
Springfield, IL 62702

Dear Dr. Sanders:

I would like to apply for the seventh grade language arts opening you have at Bentley Junior High School.

I have had more than 10 years of teaching experience at the middle school level. Currently, I teach a sixth grade self-contained class at Huntington Middle School in Peoria, but would like to concentrate on teaching the language arts. I have a master's degree in reading instruction and have established several programs at Huntington for helping reluctant students develop reading and writing skills.

Enclosed is a completed application form and a copy of my resume. I would be delighted to meet with you to further discuss my background and qualifications. You may reach me at (309) 597-9183 any time during the day. I look forward to hearing from you. Thank you for your consideration.

Sincerely,

Gene Farrell

UPDATE YOUR PLACEMENT FILE

Whether you are a novice or a veteran teacher, once you start completing job applications, it is important that you check in with the career placement center at the college from which you received your most advanced degree. The reason? To discuss, either by phone or in person, your placement file.

Your placement file is a depository for your personnel and academic data, recommendations, and student teaching/professional teaching evaluations. It is maintained by your college's career placement center and is used to support your applications for employment.

Most employers will want a copy of your placement file if you become a serious candidate. Usually this file is *closed*, which means a prospective employer has access to the file, but you do not.

Ask a career placement counselor at your college if your file is complete and up to date. If it is not, take the necessary steps to see that the file becomes complete.

Also ask the counselor to read through your file and remove any letters, evaluations, or recommendations that even hint at negativity. You might also consider removing letters or recommendations that are 10 years or older.

Special Advice on References

Be extremely selective when asking people to write references for your placement file. In most cases, you won't have a chance to review what they say about you, so you want to ask people you are confident will say good things about you. I suggest using this three-step process:

1. **Draw up a list of three to five reference candidates.** These can include education professors, teaching supervisors, or any other past employers. If you and your last employer did not get along, don't use him or her. You should have at least one contemporary on this list, but you can choose someone else who is capable of writing about your most recent work—a department head or colleague perhaps.

2. **Next, show reference candidates your Work Strengths Summary (Chapter 1).** Ask them if they would look it over and give you some feedback (i.e. , to highlight skills on the summary sheet that they think are your top strengths as well as to suggest other skills you might have omitted).

3. **Finally, evaluate responses to determine which candidates to select as references.** Use the following criteria:
   - Do not select any candidate who is unwilling to review your Work Strengths Summary. Such a person probably will not take the time to write a good letter of recommendation.
   - Also delete any person who heavily corrects your summary, offers minimal input, or seems otherwise detached from the evaluation activity.
   - Select those candidates who are enthusiastic about the skills on your summary sheet or are supportive of your goals.

FOLLOW UP YOUR APPLICATION

It's been three weeks since you sent your formal application to a prospective school. More than likely, one of the following has occurred:

Scenario #1

You received a form letter thanking you for your interest, but for one reason or another, denying you an interview.

ACTION: Send the employer a letter that: (1) thanks him or her for responding to your inquiry, (2) addresses the employer's concern about you (if the employer stated one in the letter), and (3) asks the employer to keep you in mind for future job openings or interview opportunities. Then, at least every few months, check in via follow-up call or follow-up card.

Scenario #2

You have received no response.

ACTION: Pick up the phone and follow up. Example:

Teacher: Hello, this is Maria Jones. A few months ago I applied for a teaching position in your school district. I would like very much to sit down and talk with you about the needs of your district and how my experience and skills might serve those needs.

Employer: I'm sorry, but we're very busy around here right now. There's just no time to set up an appointment. Besides, we're not really expecting any openings in the near future.

Teacher: Thank you, Dr. Smithers. I understand. May I call again in a few months to see how your needs stand then? I would very much like to work in your district. I'm particularly interested in working with reluctant learners and think your district is developing some very exciting programs in this area.

Employer: I'm glad to hear you're interested in our new education programs. I guess it couldn't hurt to check in again later.

Teacher: Thank you for your time. I'll speak with you again soon.

FOLLOW UP AGAIN

Is it all right to check back several times with employers? Absolutely! One teacher reported that she checked back once every month in the spring and once every two weeks during the summer. She reasoned that it is better to become known than forgotten. This teacher ended up getting a position that usually required a special education certificate, without having one herself! How? She continued to call back those people who seemed interested in further contact.

Here's a sample repeat call:

Teacher: Hello, this is Maria Jones. A few months ago I applied for a teaching position in your school district. At the time, there were no openings or opportunities for exploratory interviews. I'm calling to see if anything has changed. I'm still interested and available.

Employer: No, things are pretty much the same around here. I don't anticipate any changes.

Teacher: Thank you, Dr. Smithers. May I check in again in a few months? I would very much like to work in your district. As I mentioned to you before, I'm particularly interested in working with reluctant learners and think your district is developing some very exciting programs in this area.

Employer: Oh, yes. I remember you saying that. Well, I don't think the employment situation will change in the near future, but you can keep trying.

Teacher: Thank you for your time. I'll speak with you again soon.

When You Can't Get Through . . .

Sometimes you may not get through to an employer when you call to follow up. That's not always bad. It can be very helpful to get on a first-name basis with other workers in the office, and an intercepted follow-up call can give you a chance to do so. Here's a sample call that does just that:

Teacher: Hello, this is Maria Jones. May I speak with Dr. Smithers? I'm calling to see if any teaching positions or interview opportunities have opened up. I'm still interested and available.

Receptionist: Oh, hello, Maria. Dr. Smithers is out now, but I'll tell her you called.

Teacher: Thank you, Helen. I appreciate your relaying the message.

FOLLOW-UP TIP

Remember: Job vacancies often occur at odd times. One way to increase the chances that your name will surface when a sudden vacancy arises is to send prospective employers a short monthly or bimonthly note expressing your continued interest in a district or school.

STAY ORGANIZED

It is very easy to lose track of names, school addresses, interview dates, leads, and follow-up tasks. The easiest way to make your job search more organized is to complete an index card like the following for each important contact.

Review the cards each week and compile a to-do list based on your comments in the "Helpful Info" and "Follow-up" categories on the cards. Combine this list with the formal daily list found under the worksheet in Chapter 6 entitled, Job Seeker's Daily Attitude and Goal Sheet. This sheet is also used as a self-motivational tool, which is why it is presented in a later chapter.

CARD FRONT

Name: _____ Position: _____

Phone: _____ Referred By: _____

Address: _____

CALL #1: Date: _____
Purpose: _____
Helpful Info:* _____
_____
_____
Follow-Up: _____
_____
_____
_____

* Note tips offered, observations about the contact, interests of this person

CARD BACK

CALL #2: Date: _____
Purpose: _____
Helpful Info: _____
_____
_____
Follow-Up: _____
_____
_____
_____

CALL #3: Date: _____
Purpose: _____
Helpful Info: _____
_____
_____
Follow-Up: _____
_____
_____
_____

WHAT ELSE CAN I DO TO BECOME KNOWN?

I often hear job seekers say, "I've sent out my applications and requested interviews; now I don't have anything to do but wait." Not so! Take this time to become better known in a district and to demonstrate your abilities by doing these things:

- Student teach.
- Substitute teach.
  - Network with building staff.
  - Ask the principal to evaluate your teaching.
- Attend local professional conferences.
- Be active in professional organizations.
  - Help with the newsletter, conduct surveys, etc.
  - Help organize conferences, mailings, membership drives, etc.
- Volunteer in the schools.
  - Become a part-time tutor.
  - Chaperon student events.
  - Join advisory committees.
  - Participate in PTA or other parent/family organizations.
  - Work on fund-raising or bond issues.
- Acquire helpful skills or knowledge.
  - Take an education course at a nearby college or university.

MORE ON SUBSTITUTE TEACHING

In today's more competitive market, many new or returning teachers find that they cannot expect to land a full-time teaching job the first year of their search. Many of these teachers use substituting as a way to become known in a particular school or district.

One woman I know had worked for years in interior design and then decided to return to teaching when the owner of the company closed shop. Unfortunately, competition for teachers was tough in her area and she wasn't able to secure a full-time teaching job. She decided to substitute teach. She told me, "I had never seen myself as a substitute. But it is marvelous. I am now on a first-name basis with many influential supervisors.

"Substitute teaching also lets me get inside several schools, really inside, and see how things work. One school I go to has strict behavior and dress policies, another favors open-ended methods, and another focuses on an area I'd never even heard of before. This knowledge will help me with my interviews next year because I know which schools interest me and which ones I want to avoid."

The woman went on to say that she had a business card printed and leaves it with each teacher whose class she enjoys. At schools she particularly enjoys, she puts her card by the faculty room where phone lists are left. In this way, she's getting known—and also more calls for substitute jobs!

Chapter Five

MASTER THE INTERVIEW

Everything you've done so far—assessing your strengths and experiences, researching school districts, setting up a network of education contacts, putting together a strong resume, writing effective query letters, and sending in job applications, has been leading to this point: an interview with a prospective employer. No matter how superbly you performed these earlier tasks, the interview is the magic moment (actually more like 30 minutes or more) when you either sink or swim. This chapter can turn you into a master "swimmer."

KNOW THE BASICS

In this chapter, an *interview* is loosely defined as any opportunity you have to describe your talents to a person with hiring authority.

Types of Interviews

There are many types of interview formats. There is the *casual interview* that takes place during a professional conference. An administrator asks you about your interests and experiences. Then you get his or her card and an invitation to visit the district. These do happen and they are fun.

There is the *single person* interview where you answer questions one on one. Most of the time you will be interviewed by a person who has direct hiring authority. However, you may be interviewed by a personnel specialist or by another person in the school district whose judgment is respected by the hiring authority. In this case, you are probably undergoing a special type of single person interview called a *screening interview*, which is designed solely to pare down the number of candidates appropriate for the position. If you pass the screening, you'll be called back for more interviewing.

There is also the *group or committee interview*. This type has several variations. In most cases, you will interview with one or more persons individually and then speak with a larger group. This type of interview can be quite taxing because it takes several hours and by the end many people will have cross-examined you with both the same and different questions. The best approach is to remain focused: listen carefully, think before you react, ask an interviewer to clarify a question when you are unsure about its answer, and try to keep your answers decisive and consistent.

Finally, there is the *multi-stage interview* where you first meet a committee or individual and, if successful, you work your way through a series of interviews scheduled during a period of several weeks.

Stages of an Interview

Regardless of type, the interview usually unfolds in three or four logical stages.

First Stage

During the first stage, the agenda focuses on getting acquainted with you and building rapport. Interviewers try to get you to open up. The questions are general in nature about why you got into teaching, where you have lived, and your goals.

The most common opener is: "Tell me about yourself." What the interviewer really wants to know is: Who are you and what can you do for my school district? This question deserves some advance work. Prepare an answer by comparing the strengths and accomplishments you listed on your Work Strengths Summary with the objectives of the district. Your response should tell the interviewer why he or she should hire you over several other candidates who may appear equally qualified.

Second Stage

During the second stage, you will be asked general questions related to your experience in the field of education. These questions usually call upon your knowledge of basic methods and interpersonal skills.

Third Stage

The third stage probes deeper. These are questions of a technical or more specific nature. They can range from: "Do you know how to use a computer to calculate grades?" to "How have you used direct instruction methods?"

Another type of question in the third stage is the open-ended situational question that might sound like: "What would you do if two students get in a fight?"

Then the interviewer might probe for problems in your background by asking:"Why did you leave your last job?" or "How did you feel about your district when it cut vocational programs?" or "Why did you give up the department chair position?" or "How do you feel about traveling between two schools?" or the real clincher, "What do you think about your most recent boss?"

The rule in any discussion about bosses is obviously never to criticize one. By criticizing a boss, you may be giving the impression that you lack the interpersonal skills necessary to work closely with others.

One other probing question worth discussing is: "What don't you do well?" In your reply to this question, you should never say anything negative about yourself. Have an answer prepared that actually reveals a strength. You have only 20 to 30 minutes in a job interview to convince a prospective employer you are right for the job, so you don't want to provide information that may say you are not.

A good answer for "What don't you do well?" might be:

"Working in isolation. I like to be with people." This actually indicates a positive trait in the field of education because working with others is what education is all about."

Fourth Stage

In closing, you may be asked if *you* have any questions. This is a great opportunity to demonstrate your interest in the district with questions such as: "Do you plan on continuing the talented and gifted program I have read about?" and " Do you see any chance for me to play a role in this program?"

You might also use the time to cover some experiences and knowledge you haven't been able to work into the interview. For example, you might ask: "How do you feel about metacognitive approaches?" or "Would my experience in alternative education be useful in your district?"

PRACTICE, PRACTICE PRACTICE

The best way to excel at interviewing is to practice. Following is a list of frequently asked questions. In your mind, decide how to answer them. Remember that your goal is to be concise and consistent. For questions you think you might have difficulty handling, actually write out a response and practice saying it. The object is not to memorize an answer, but to become comfortable addressing a specific issue. You want to sound articulate, but not coached.

Once you feel comfortable addressing all of the questions, role play an interview with a friend. Your friend should ask each question on the list and you should respond accordingly. Tape-record your answers and listen to see if you sound confident and convincing. Revise and practice your answers until you do.

Rapport-Building Questions

- Won't you tell me about yourself?
- Why did you decide on a career in education?
- What do you like best about your work? What least? Why?
- Why do you think you are qualified for this job?
- Why do you want to work for us?
- Do you have any hobbies or special talents that could enhance this job?
- In what additional areas could you contribute? For example, in what extracurricular activities could you demonstrate leadership?

General Experience Questions

- How would you evaluate student progress?
- How would you describe your ideal administrator?
- What is the best role for a parent to play in the school district?
- How can you structure a class in subject x so that you afford maximum teacher/student contact?
- What general strategies do you use when encountering students who exhibit anti-social behavior?
- What was your last classroom challenge and how did you meet it?
- What is your philosophy of education?

Technical Questions

- What type of discipline method do you prefer?
- Can you operate a computer?
- How would you use cooperative learning strategies to teach subject x?
- What's your experience with paperwork like IEPs?

Situational Questions

- Do you involve students in making rules?
- Is it important to be liked by students?
- Is it important to be liked by colleagues?
- If a student found a quarter in your classroom what would you do?
- If a student was disrupting your class or lesson what would you do?
- How do you group students for instruction?
- What do you do when you disagree with another teacher's approach?
- How would you handle a disruptive student?
- What would you do with a noncompliant student?
- How do you handle parents who are angry?
- How do you know when a lesson was well done?
- Are you familiar with ITIP? Consult Models? Peer Tutoring? (etc.)
- Suppose after a personal talk a student reveals some personal concerns, then withdraws from you later. What would you do?
- Can a teacher be too involved with students? Why?

- Suppose you suspect a child is a victim of abuse, but your past attempts to get support from administrators have not been successful. What would you do?

Probing Questions

- What are your professional plans five years from now?

- Why did you leave teaching?
- Why have you changed jobs so often?
- Why did you leave your last job?
- How well did you get along with your past supervisor?
- What do you think about your most recent boss?
- What would be an ideal job for you?
- What don't you do well?

DON'T LEAVE HOME WITHOUT THESE PREPARATIONS

If you have done your homework up to this point (i.e., developed a good resume and practiced answering typical interview questions) your last-minute interview preparations can be reduced to two decisions: What should I bring to the interview and what should I wear?

Bring These Things:

Before you leave for your interview, check to see that you are armed with the following materials:

- **Resume.** Take several copies of your resume. (There may be more than one person interviewing you who would like a copy.) Also, be sure you have edited your resume to reflect the specific needs of the job opening you are applying for and your ability to fulfill those needs.
- **Letters of Reference.** In most cases, you will not need to supply letters of reference during your interview. But if you have them at your disposal, bring them along. They may help you to make a point about your abilities or background.
- **Questions to Ask.** Write these questions in advance on note cards and stash them in your purse or pocket for easy and discrete access.
- **Portfolio of Your Work.** If you have hard-core evidence of your achievements, by all means bring it along in the form of a personal portfolio. Your portfolio could include outlines of unusual lessons you created, articles about educational programs you initiated, photographs of school events you managed, and so on.

Dress for Success

Dress as though you worked in the school district and were receiving visitors. People (prospective employers) are automatically drawn to those who are like themselves. If you are unsure how people dress, visit the district. If you can't visit, then call and ask a secretary for advice. Don't wear anything overly trendy or ultra-fashionable. You are safest erring on the side of conservatism.

Little touches can make a big difference as well. Don't leave home without shined shoes, manicured fingernails, and neatly combed hair.

LET YOUR PERSONAL BEST SHINE THROUGH

There are lots of job-search books on the market that provide their own personalized laundry lists of interview do's and don'ts. These lists can be overwhelming. For that reason, I'll restrain myself and provide you with the most important do's. Do:

- **Plan to arrive at the interview site at least 10 minutes early.** Give yourself at least that amount of time to avoid any mishaps. Wait in your car or walk around the block so that you arrive at the interviewer's reception area a just few minutes ahead of schedule. Such promptness suggests you are a responsible worker.
- **Develop an impressive introductory handshake.** If you are uncomfortable with handshakes, practice until it seems second nature. Practice looking the person in the eye, grasping the hand firmly, while saying the person's name. Then try to use this person's name in conversation as soon as you can. Realize that employers are nervous just like job seekers. Be yourself and try to project your natural charm, warmth, and good-natured enthusiasm. Remember that a smile will work wonders in putting both you and the interviewer at ease.
- **Listen carefully to each interview question before you respond.** You don't want to miss the subtle intent of the question.
- **Keep criticisms of previous employers and teachers to yourself.** This type of negativity may suggest to the interviewer that you lack important interpersonal skills.
- **Concentrate on the positive.** When discussing past problems, concentrate on how you overcame the barriers and grew as an individual.
- **Use direct eye contact.** As you listen to someone speak, place visual emphasis on that speaker, but still scan about. This shows that you are listening intently but does not give the speaker the feeling you are staring. Be sure to maintain that good eye contact as you speak. You'll give the impression you are providing honest and forthright information. If you are shy, then try looking at a person's forehead instead of directly into his or her eyes. (No one will know the difference!)
- **Try to inject your knowledge of the district and community into your interview.** This information can come from visiting, reading newspapers, reading district pamphlets, and visiting the Chamber of Commerce. The information should suggest that you will enjoy working in the community and are aware of the community's assets. Be prepared to explain why you feel living and working in the school district will meet your needs. Small districts especially want to know if applicants have ever lived in rural or small towns before.
- **Don't be afraid of honesty.** If you absolutely do not know an answer to a question, simply admit it and suggest how you might find the answer. For example you might say: "I've never used peer tutoring before, but I know who to contact at the local teachers' college to find out more." This shows you are a problem solver.
- **If you are unsure about an answer to a question, ask the interviewer if he or she can rephrase it.** This gives you time to think. Plus, when asked to rephrase a question the interviewer will often include hints. If you are unsure if your answer was adequate, or if the listener seems concerned or confused, stop and ask: "Have I answered the question to your satisfaction? Would you like any additional information?"

GO FOR THE STRONG FINISH

Ending the interview is like ending a first date that you enjoyed. You don't want to just fade away in the mind of the other person; you want to make a lasting impression. Close your interview with a firm handshake, direct eye contact, and a statement that sums up your interest in and suitability for the position. Let's examine this advice:

1. **Explicitly state your interest.** Employers often comment on a candidate's successful interview and then remark: "I wonder if he/she wants the job?" Make sure you actually say you are interested in working in the district. This is particularly important if you have asked some probing questions of your own that suggest you have specific concerns and expectations. A simple, "I would enjoy being a _____ in this school district," will suffice.

2. **Summarize your top three to five strengths.** During an interview many things are discussed. It is easy to lose focus. A brief summary gives the interviewer a final snapshot or review picture of you. It could sound like: "I think that I would fit in well here because of my previous experience in driver's education and my work with slow learners. I am also interested in coaching and youth clubs."

3. **Thank the interviewer and ask about the next step in the interviewing process or suggest a next step.** Say something like: "I want to thank you for your time. I've enjoyed meeting you and learning more about your district." Then add: "What will be the next step be in the interviewing process?" or "May I check back with you next month to see how things are going?"

EVALUATE THE INTERVIEW

The following checklist can help you evaluate your job interview. Be sure to do this no later than a day or two after the interview while events are still fresh in your mind. This evaluation serves two purposes: (1) it can help you determine follow-up strategies what you can do to further convince the interviewer that you are right for the job and (2) it can help you polish your interviewing technique for interviews at other school districts.

As you run through this checklist, remind yourself that everyone makes mistakes especially in the early interviewing stage. In fact, that is why I always advise job seekers to conduct their first interviews with their second or third place choices. A little practice and some careful evaluation can go a long way toward turning yourself into a skillful interviewee.

Was I Prepared?
❑ I knew enough about the district and the community.
❑ I brought the right materials (resume, samples of my work, etc).
❑ My dress and appearance were appropriate.
❑ I knew about the job being interviewed.

How Was My Interview Performance?
❑ My posture showed interest, not nervousness or apathy.
❑ My eye contact was good.
❑ My introductions went smoothly.
❑ I remembered the names of most people.
❑ I was enthusiastic without being too aggressive.
❑ I listened well without interrupting or answering too quickly.
❑ I did not talk too much.
❑ I spoke loudly and clearly.
❑ I smiled a lot. (People remember those who smile.)
❑ I was prepared for most of the questions.

❑ I asked good questions.
❑ I was courteous to everyone I met including secretaries.

Something I did that caused the employer to look concerned was:

_____
_____
_____

Some new questions I should add to my list to prepare for are:

_____
_____
_____

Some personal behaviors I might want to change are:

_____
_____
_____

Something I really felt good about was when I:

_____
_____
_____

Something I really liked about this employer was his or her:

_____
_____
_____

Did I End The Interview Properly?
❑ I closed the interview summarizing my interests and talents.

FOLLOW-UP

After you've completed an interview and evaluated your performance, it's time to start thinking about follow-up. Don't believe people who tell you a follow-up phone call or letter is unnecessary or outdated. It is your last chance to convince an interviewer that you are right for the job.

Follow-up Letters

In most cases, a follow-up letter is better than a follow-up phone call. A phone call may catch an interviewer at an awkward time and hence the conversation might not go as well as planned. A letter, on the other hand, is almost always reviewed at the interviewer's convenience.

The sooner you write and send a follow-up letter the better. An effective letter follows these three steps:

1. Begin by reminding the prospective employer of your interview.

2. Sell yourself one more time by repeating your qualifications and a highlight or two of the interview.

3. Then thank the interviewer for his or her time and restate your interest in the position.

(See sample follow-up letter on the next page.)

SAMPLE FOLLOW-UP LETTER

Sonia Parker
44 Elm St.
Vicksburg, MS 39181

January 7, 1993

Dr. Terry Fox
Superintendent
Tupelo School District
Tupelo, MS 38802

Dear Dr. Fox:

Thank you for meeting with me today to discuss the position you have available for a fifth grade language arts teacher. I was especially interested in your comments about the need to improve students' writing skills.

As I mentioned during our conversation, I have a proven track record in teaching process writing skills to students. I was happy to hear you have IBM computers available because, in the past, my most effective writing instruction used word-processing software to publish a school newspaper. I would be very interested in initiating a similar project with your fifth graders.

Again, many thanks for your time and attention. There is no doubt in my mind that I would enjoy working in the Tupelo School District. I look forward to hearing from you in the near future.

Sincerely,

Sonia Parker

Follow-Up Phone Calls

There are a few exceptions to the letter-is-better rule. Consider using the phone if:

- you have additional information or ideas you would like to share with the interviewer,
- you haven't heard anything from the interviewer in several weeks,
- you've gotten another job offer and you need to know where you stand before you make a decision, or
- your interview went badly and you would like to ask for a second interview.

Your phone call should follow the same steps as an effective letter: (1) remind the prospective employer of your interview, (2) sell yourself by repeating your qualifications and a highlight or two of the interview, and then (3) thank the interviewer for his or her time and restate your interest in the position.

Following is a sample follow-up call.

> "Mr. Fox? This is Sonia Parker. We met four weeks ago on September 15, to discuss the fifth grade language arts position you have available. I wanted to know if you've reached a decision yet. . . ."

Optional Additions:

> "Since we met, I've outlined a few ideas for implementing a school-wide writing program that you might find useful."

Or:

> "Is there anything else you would like to know about me that might help you make your decision?"

Or:

> "I've received another job offer, but before I make a decision, I'd like to know where I stand with your district."

Optional Replacement for Last Line in Original:

> "I don't feel our interview provided an accurate picture of my potential. I wondered if I might stop by to talk with you again."

One last note about follow-up calls: Be prepared for rejection. An employer may tell you right on the phone that he or she hired someone else.

If you're brave enough, politely ask why someone else was chosen instead. Ask about areas you might take a course in or other ways you might improve your chances of getting another job in the district.

Then ask if you may check back in six months to see if there are other openings. Finally, ask if the employer can refer you to job openings in another district with similar goals and values.

Chapter Six

MAINTAIN A WINNING ATTITUDE

Each day hundreds of job seekers say, "I can't find a job," and quit looking. In fact, after only one week of a search, the average adult starts slowing down the effort to only one to four hours a week. The average high school student quits looking after hearing "no" four times.

The biggest problem for most job seekers is that they can say the words "I can't" much quicker than the words "I can." Your next goal is to ensure that you become and remain an "I can" person.

YOUR ATTITUDE IS A TERRIBLE THING TO WASTE

Author Napoleon Hill studied rich and powerful people to find out how they turned their lives into success stories. In his book, *Think and Grow Rich*, he claims that whether these persons started in a big house or a small hut, all of them had one thing in common: Their attitudes were driven by their positive beliefs.

Hill discovered that the mind is like a garden. It can grow weeds or flowers. Weeds grow from seeds of despair. Flowers grow from positive thoughts. I think this analogy applies particularly well to job seekers.

When a job seeker believes that he or she can't interview very well, or has no skills, then anger grows like a weed patch. Soon the job seeker figures, "What's the use?"

The person begins searching fewer and fewer hours each day, doesn't bother to get dressed up for interviews, and generally feels everyone else gets the breaks. In the end, this person is merely going through the job-search motions. The mind is now so cluttered with weeds, the person never believes that the flower of a good job will ever blossom.

If your brain continually plants weed seeds by emitting the message, "I cannot get a job," the entire world will begin to hear this message, and you will stay unemployed longer.

To sow flower seeds, your attitude must be positive and focused upon a plan or purpose. Start each day believing that you will get a job. This thought will energize your whole attitude. When you believe in yourself, you will start your job search early, get dressed, and begin making plans. You will begin to attract positive people and situations. You are still going to hear "no" frequently, but you must believe that a "yes" is also part of your life.

In the words of Napolean Hill:

The thoughts we feed our mind
Create the energy we find.
Persistence, luck, and this energy
Create our final destiny.

PICK A DREAM TO LIVE BY

When your whole being aches with the desire for a dream to come true, you will find the impetus to think positively.

So pick a dream job you can truly strive for. Pick a dream worthy of your precious time and energy. Be future-oriented about this. Your dream job doesn't have to be your very next job; it may be something you work toward. This dream must be special if it is help you overcome disappointment and discouragement. Get power from this special thought by spending time each day thinking about your dream job. Daydream about it in your spare moments. Realize that your next job will start you on the road to your ideal job.

As you see it coming true in your mind, you will find yourself doing everything you can to make it come true in your daily life. It will become like a fire that cannot be extinguished. Then the habit of this dream takes on its own power and sweeps aside all opposition.

WHAT DO YOU DO WHEN YOU HEAR THE WORD "NO"?

Job-search experts claim that you will probably hear at least 15 to 20 "no's" or rejections before you hear a "yes" to come in and discuss a job opening.

Then, the average person hears at least three "no's" from interviewers before he or she is offered a job. That means the average person will hear from 15 to 60 "no's" before getting a job offer.

The "I Can" person makes a game out of this. So can you, with the help of the Job-Search Scorecard below. Make a copy and paste it onto a 3 × 5 index card. Carry it with you during your job search. Each time you hear a "no" use a pencil to darken out a circled "no." Then record the total number of "no's" on your Job Seeker's Daily Attitude and Goals Sheet (next page).

MY JOB-SEARCH SCORECARD

No	No	No	No	No	No	No	No
No	No	No	No	No	No	No	YES

After you darken out a "no," feed your spirit positive thoughts by saying:
I'm one more "no" closer to a "yes!"

JOB SEEKER'S DAILY ATTITUDE AND GOAL SHEET

Reinforce your winning attitude and job-search goals by completing a sheet like the following each day.

State What You Want

I want a job that

_____

_____

_____

Plan Your Efforts

To get this job, I am willing to commit my greatest energy and effort to job hunting. I will plan today to undertake these (check off items and indicate amounts in blanks):

❑ Read want ads and career-placement bulletins.
❑ Visit ____ places with job listings, such as placement offices, education departments in universities, school-district personnel, and special education offices.
❑ Call ____ administrators, teachers, or department heads.
❑ Network with ____ persons about job leads.
❑ Visit a school in a district where I want to work.
❑ Complete and return ____ job applications.
❑ Write ____ letters to prospective employers.
❑ Write thank-you letters to ____ recent interviewers or ____ job-opening contacts.
❑ Join and participate in professional organizations.
❑ Join and participate in school/community groups.
❑ Sign up to substitute in this district: _____ .
❑ Conduct a career survey in a place I typically don't visit, such as a state agency, a place where grants are allocated, or a professional organization.
❑ Rewrite my resume or write a new one featuring:

_____

_____

_____

End Your Day By Reviewing Your Efforts

1. I got closer to the "yes" by getting this many "no's":

_____

2. An example of my energy, persistence, and effort was when I:

_____

_____

_____

3. Review each item you checked off on the list at left. Circle each one that you completed today. Assign any you did not complete to one of the To-Do lists below.

_____

_____

_____

4. Something I need to learn more about is:

_____

_____

_____

5. I am a winner. Tomorrow I will begin the day with this thought:

_____

_____

TO DO IMMEDIATELY:

_____

_____

_____

TO DO IN THE FUTURE:

_____

_____

_____

_____

THE ULTIMATE JOB-SEARCH LIST

When nothing seems to be working, check to see that you are concentrating on what is really important. Review these job-search essentials. If you are not using them, do so immediately!

❑ **Use many methods of job search.** Experts say that the more methods you use, the quicker you will find work. Use as many methods as you can from the Job Seeker's Daily Attitude and Goal Sheet (previous page).

❑ **Visit persons in your field weekly or monthly.** They don't all have to be prospective employers. They may be job counselors, school secretaries, anyone who will talk to you about your job search.

❑ **Check back with school districts that interest you three times even if you are told there are no foreseeable openings.** Everything changes from week to week. People leave, levies fail and even more educators leave, grant monies come in, a person gets pregnant, another person get's injured, somebody takes early retirement, another person gets promoted leaving an opening behind, someone goes back to school, etc., etc. . . . Check back three times. Don't apologize, just say how much you really want to work in that district. Also check back several times with your contacts in the field to see if they have any new job leads.

❑ **Dress for success each day.** Getting dressed up puts you in the right frame of mind. Dress as though you might bump into an employer. Make people think that you are somebody on the move. If you dress shabbily, you'll get only shabby help from contacts you meet. Everyone wants to help a winner.

❑ **Get out and meet people.** Don't just sit and wait to be called by personnel departments that have your application. Don't wait for job openings to miraculously appear on the job board of your choice. Use your networking skills to estimate where the desirable openings will be. Dig in and learn all you can about these school districts and the people who run them. Then make yourself visible in these districts and to these people. Conduct school surveys, substitute teach, volunteer for school-related projects

❑ **Tell everyone you meet about your job hunt.** You never know who may lead you to that long-awaited "yes."

❑ **Take time out for your leisure life.** All workers get time off, and job-hunting is hard work. Reward yourself. You've earned it!

Chapter Seven

EVALUATE YOUR OFFERS

Now that you have an offer (or maybe two or three offers) how will you respond? Treat this step of the job search as carefully as you treated all of the other steps. Instead of saying "yes" or "no" immediately to any employer, thank him or her in an enthusiastic manner and ask for a day or two to consider the opportunity.

IS THIS AN OFFER YOU CAN'T REFUSE?

Use the following checklist to help you evaluate an offer or compare more than one offer. For each numbered question below, check "yes" or "no." Then focus on the items most important to you. If you give a school more than two "no's" on items important to you, think twice before joining that faculty!

CHECK ONE:
YES NO

Is the School Right for Me?

❑ ❑ 1. Will I enjoy the community setting (the lifestyle, socializing opportunities, and location)?

❑ ❑ 2. Are the school facilities adequate? (This includes classrooms, storage areas, teaching tools and resources, faculty room, and general architecture.)

❑ ❑ 3. Is the average pupil-teacher ratio and total school population agreeable to me?

❑ ❑ 4. Will I be comfortable with the staff's level of involvement and its personality makeup?

❑ ❑ 5. Does the school's management style, in particular, its decision-making process, reflect my own management style and expectations?

❑ ❑ 6. Will I enjoy working with the principal (or other supervisor)?

❑ ❑ 7. Do I agree with the school's philosophical direction—its educational beliefs, strategies, and goals?

❑ ❑ 8. Does the school have a good reputation?

CHECK ONE:
YES NO

Is the Position Right for Me?

❑ ❑ 9. Are the job requirements compatible with my work skill, strengths, and experiences?

❑ ❑ 10. Will the position interest me on a day-to-day basis?

❑ ❑ 11. Will the position broaden my work experience? Will it lead to other career alternatives?

❑ ❑ 12. Will I enjoy working with the students that this job is designed to serve?

❑ ❑ 13. Will I enjoy working with their learning styles, age range, scholastic abilities, etc.?

❑ ❑ 14. Will I find the additional obligations and expectations of the job (i.e. extracurricular responsibilities, committee work, etc.) challenging?

Are the Salary and Benefits Right for Me?

❑ ❑ 15. Is the salary adequate? Is it competitive with state standards? Will it allow me to live comfortably?

❑ ❑ 16. Are health benefits adequate?

❑ ❑ 17. Are dental benefits adequate?

❑ ❑ 18. Are life insurance benefits adequate?

❑ ❑ 19. Is the retirement package acceptable?

❑ ❑ 20. Is the time-off acceptable? (Time-off includes vacation days, holidays, sick days, personal days, and maternity days.)

Delay, If You Must

Suppose you have one offer, but you really want a job in another school/district. It is perfectly acceptable to take a few more days before giving an answer to the second choice employer.

If you sense that an explanation is in order, be truthful. Tell the employer who made you an offer that you have not yet concluded employment discussions with another school/district and that you need a little time before you can adequately evaluate all of your opportunities. The time you can reasonably ask for varies with the needs of specific employers and the time of the year. At the early part of summer, you might get up to three weeks; while near the end of summer, you might get only a few days.

Next, call your first choice school/district and let the employer know your general situation (try to avoid mentioning specifics about the other job opportunity). Then ask if he or she expects to make a decision within the time period you have been allotted by the other employer. If the answer is "yes," hang in there; if it's "no," and you feel you can't buy any more time from your second choice, you'll have to decide between a definite job offer and a indefinite, yet more preferable, one.

Sign On The Dotted Line . . . Carefully

In most cases, when you accept a job in education, you will be asked to sign an employment contract. Signing a contract is a professional and legal commitment. If you try to break it later, the district may take you to court or try to have your certification revoked. Only sign a contract you intend to keep. Contracts can be broken for legitimate personal hardships such as illness, a spouse being transferred, or unexpected family obligations. But trying to get out of one contract and into another may result in your losing both contracts.

APPENDIX A:
TIPS FOR COLLEGE AND UNIVERSITY JOB-SEEKERS

The general process remains the same for any job search in education. However, some rituals of the search may differ. Following are rituals specific to educators who seek positions at the college and university level.

Researching Target Schools

First of all, searches usually involve long-distance job seeking. When you apply to places far away, the mail becomes very important. Use it to obtain college catalogs, department handouts to current students, papers published by faculty members or those who might end up interviewing you, and local newspapers and college papers.

Be sure to read your professional journals with a specific eye on new trends. These also list openings because most employers use the advertising listing to meet affirmative action goals.

Networking is important, too. You can almost always find someone who knows someone who works at a school you are interested in. Each field is small and tightly knit. Try to attend as many professional conferences as you can in order to pick up on trends and meet people. Be sure to attend the social functions of each conference and bring along resumes and a contact card.

Your best guide, however, will be a mentor who works in the field. Work closely with your major professor or an influential colleague to learn about current hiring practices and see if he or she knows anyone in the places you want to apply.

More Paperwork—The Vita

In many cases, you may need a *vita* instead of a resume. (A prepared job seeker at the college and university level has one of each.) A vita is like an extended resume. It covers many of the same categories, such as career objective, education summary, and work summary, but it also lists, usually under a subhead such as Professional and Creative Works, your professional contributions and involvements. Look at samples from colleagues or ask your placement office for samples. I suggest you include the following types of information under Professional and Creative Works (or a similar major subhead):

- *Personal Publications:* Provide bibliographic data on all citations, pamphlets, monographs, chapters in books, books, articles, and research reports.

- *Papers Presented:* For each paper, list its title, the conference where it was presented, and the date and location of the conference. Also note invited and competitive entries for each conference.

- *Professional Service:* List by name and date, all organizational memberships, positions on boards, reviewing or editing responsibilities, committee work, recitals, performances, exhibits, and consulting and advisory work.

- *Past and Current Research:* Identify objective(s) of all research projects as well as their time periods.

Interview Rituals

The interview process at the college and university level can be more elaborate. It often involves three levels: a demonstration, some socializing, and several meetings with various staff members. The demonstration will usually require you to deliver a lecture to staff or students. The socializing will be at a party or luncheon where staff can mingle and get to know you. The meetings will consist of a variety of interviews. (See Chapter 6 for more on interview formats.)

If you are offered a position during the interview process, bear in mind that you don't have to reject or accept it immediately. If salary is a problem, suggest something that pegs your interest between theirs. For example, if they offer $20,000–$25,000, you can respond with, "Yes, between 22 and 28 would be acceptable."

Finally, if your interview is out of town, try to arrive the day before. You'll need to be rested and acclimated.

APPENDIX B:
OVERSEAS TEACHING JOBS

Have you ever considered teaching overseas? There are many opportunities to explore and just as many "scams"—newsletters, job lists, reports, and so on, being sold around these opportunities. Joyce Lain Kennedy, author of the Los Angles Time Syndicate's column CAREERS and senior author of the bestseller *Joyce Lain Kennedy's Career Book*, summarizes what to look for in terms of resources and scams in the following response to a reader of her syndicated column. One newsletter she recommends, *International Employment Hotline*, includes not only job possibilities, but also typical stories about teachers who get jobs overseas. These stories help you understand the human side of teaching abroad.

Dear Joyce;

Two questions for you: How do I get a teaching job overseas and what about those publications listing jobs overseas?

—H.R.S.

The last question first because of the rip-off threat to many people. Many, perhaps most, newsletters claiming to report on global employment are junk mail. Too good to be true. Among the sterling exceptions is the respected, no-hype *International Employment Hotline*, published by Will Cantrell. Even that is being counterfeited by an intellectual property thief in Amsterdam, Holland.

The counterfeit piece uses the name, logo, masthead statement ("Celebrating our 14th Year of Reporting on the International Job Market") and slogan ("Discover What's Waiting for You in the World—and How to Get It Now!"). The map and list of countries covered was copied from a direct mail piece Cantrell used about four years ago, and the remainder is a total "come on" with no relation to the true nature of the international job market. The counterfeiter's list of testimonials at the back appears to be bogus. The whole thing is a cheap imitation with the potential to damage the real *International Employment Hotline*.

So, what can Cantrell do about it? "Not much," he says, "other than to plod along with my attorney. I'm concerned about the damage to our name, Long after the culprit has folded his tent and gone on to the next scam, I'll be battling the image he left behind."

Cantrell is an old travel hand who has built up his business by honest labor for more than a dozen years. He's being victimized. The public is being victimized. And unless Cantrell is able to spend megabucks with big international law firms, he appears to be stalled, and perhaps stymied. I anticipate this type of thievery happening more and more as business goes global.

In the meantime, if you want a subscription to the honest product, drop Cantrell an inquiry note at Worldwise Books, Box 3030, Oakton, VA 22124.

On a happier note, the latest copy of *Overseas Employment Opportunities for Educators* is available free from the Department of Defense, Office of Dependent Schools, 2461 Eisenhower Ave., Alexandria, VA 22331; 703-325-0867. The publication tells you about teaching jobs in 250 schools operated for children of U.S. military and civilian personnel stationed overseas. You usually need to qualify in two subject areas. Pay ranges from about $22,500 to $38,100 annually.

Another resource: Teacher Exchange Branch, Office of International Education, U.S. Department of Education, Washington, D.C. 20202; 202-708-7283.

The second edition of a nice little guide, *How to Find Jobs Teaching Overseas* by James Muckle, gives you a feel for the adventure. The plain-spoken writer has taught his way around the world, and his book is in part a useful autobiography and part a resource listing of agencies to contact for global educational opportunities. Muckle's book is like a chat with an old friend who tells you what it's really like. Get the privately published book for $7.95 from KSJ Publishing Co., Box 2311, Sebastopol, CA 95473.

Timing is important when seeking an overseas teaching position. The season is from November to March each year. If you don't have a job by April, you'd better plan on the following academic year.

© 1992 Sun Features, Inc./distributed by Los Angeles Times Syndicate.

APPENDIX C:
BIBLIOGRAPHY

Allen, Jeffery G. *How to Turn an Interview Into a Job*, New York: Simon and Schuster, Inc., 1983.

Bolles, Richard Nelson. *How to Create a Picture of Your Ideal Job or Next Career*, Berkeley, Calif.: Ten Speed Press, 1989.

Bolles, Richard Nelson. *What Color Is Your Parachute?*, Berkeley, Calif.: Ten Speed Press, 1993.

Bloomberg, Gerri, and Holden, Margaret. *The Women's Job Search Handbook*, Charlotte, Vir.: Williamson Publishing, 1991.

Faux, Marian. *The Complete Resume Book*, New York: Prentice Hall, 1991.

Kennedy, Joyce Lain, and Laramore, Darryl. *Career Book*, Lincolnwood, Ill.: VGM Career Horizons, 1992.

Ross, Kathryn and Ross. *The Only Job Hunting Guide You'll Ever Need*, New York: Poseidon Press, 1989.